LITTLE GREEN
R E A D E R S

American Buffalo

Focus: Endangered Animals

Meredith Costain

American buffalo are big animals. They have sharp horns and long, shaggy fur.

American buffalo live on flat lands called plains. They eat grass and small plants. They live in groups called herds.

Buffalo can weigh more than horses and cows. They can be friendly to people, live in corrals, and eat hay like horses and cows.

Buffalo are at risk.
Many years ago, settlers
hunted them. They killed
one million buffalo
each year to make
room for new homes.
Because herds
of buffalo travel very
slowly, settlers killed
lots of buffalo
at one time.

Before the settlers came, 60 million buffalo lived in the United States and Canada. One hundred years later, only about 1,000 buffalo were still living.

Now, people have set aside reservations and preserves where buffalo herds can live and grow. Seventy-five thousand buffalo are alive today.

Some buffalo live in the wild in national parks. People can visit the parks and learn how to protect buffalo.

Index